For Hannah, Jacob, Maya, Sara, Bennett, Eli, and Noa,
who always sit still for a wild tale
G. A.

For Jacob, Lizzy, Sarah, and Charlie
K. O.

Text copyright © 2007 by Gail Ablow
Illustrations copyright © 2007 by Kathy Osborn

First edition 2007

Library of Congress Cataloging-in-Publication Data is available.

Library of Congress Catalog Card Number 2006051855

ISBN 978-0-7636-2838-3

2 4 6 8 10 9 7 5 3 1

Printed in Singapore

This book was typeset in Cushing.
The illustrations were done in gouache.

Candlewick Press
2067 Massachusetts Avenue
Cambridge, Massachusetts 02140

visit us at www.candlewick.com

A HORSE IN THE HOUSE

and Other Strange But True Animal Stories

GAIL ABLOW   illustrated by KATHY OSBORN

CANDLEWICK PRESS
CAMBRIDGE, MASSACHUSETTS

INTRODUCTION

This is a book of true animal stories from the news. Many of these stories are hard to believe. That's because we're people. We get used to animals—and ourselves—acting in predictable ways. So prepare to be surprised by our feathered, furry, and scaly neighbors—how they're built, how they act, and just how smart they can be.

The facts in these stories were all found in news reports from around the world. If you are curious about where the stories were first reported, there is a list of sources at the end of the book. Although the stories are true, we do depart from fact in some ways: the pictures are colorful flights of fancy, and as to what these animals were thinking—sometimes we can only imagine. No animals were actually interviewed for this book.

Overall, we were struck by what happens when people and animals interact—how sensible animals are, and how silly or extravagant people can be, even when they mean well. Should donkeys get married? Should cats be made to spy? We may all have different opinions. We hope you have fun reading these amazing true tales, learning about behavior (both animal and human), and sharing what you think—politely—without baring your claws or showing your teeth.

THE GREEN RABBIT

France is known for artists who like to experiment. Monet painted pictures of haystacks with colors as pink as cotton candy. Picasso sculpted faces that look like crumpled paper bags. "That's not art!" the art critics yelled . . . until they changed their minds. Art sometimes helps people see the world differently.

That's what artist Eduardo Kac of Chicago hoped to do. He wanted to create art that was surprising and new, even if people yelled at him. Instead of paints and brushes, Eduardo borrowed his tools from science. Instead of working in a studio, he used a laboratory. Eduardo the artist wanted to make a rabbit—a real and very different rabbit. It wouldn't be easy.

Eduardo asked French scientists for help. The scientists copied a special jellyfish gene that makes it glow green in the dark of the sea. Genes, like special operating instructions, help tell bodies how to work. The scientists then put the green gene into a baby bunny growing inside a mother rabbit. When that bunny was born in the lab, Eduardo, his wife, and his daughter named her Alba.

Alba looks ordinary at first: white and plump, with a twinkle in her red eyes. But shine a special light at Alba, and like a jellyfish, she glows green: green fur, green whiskers, bright apple-green eyes. It was love at first sight for Eduardo.

Eduardo says Alba is "gentle" and "charming." But is she art?

The head scientist says absolutely not; she's a science experiment and must stay in the lab. Alba is art, protests Eduardo, who thinks she should live with his family. When news of Alba spread around the world, no one could agree whether scientists or artists should make green-glowing rabbits at all.

Eduardo's wife, Ruth, and daughter, Miriam, are very sad. They don't care whether Alba is labeled art or not. They just want her to come home and be their pet. As for Alba, who remains in a French lab, she is content to be cuddled by scientists or artists—as long as they feed her lettuce and carrots and treat her like the queen of green.

THE DONKEY WEDDING

Near the Indian city of Bangalore, people were waiting for rain. It
was monsoon season, and they needed the drenching storms to fill the
rivers and lakes, water the crops, and clean the dusty streets. This June,
however, not a single raindrop fell from the sunny sky. Every day people
searched for clouds and saw nothing but blue. They grew grumpy . . .
then *grumpier.*

Finally, in a tiny village called Magadi, the people decided to hold a
donkey wedding. They cooked up a feast of sweets and sent out a hundred
invitations. According to Hindu legend, a water god named Varuna once
gave a donkey the power to find water. The villagers hoped that honoring
a donkey couple would inspire Varuna to make it rain.

They named the donkey bride Ganga after a holy river and the
donkey groom Varuna after the water god himself. Ganga looked lovely
in her wedding sari, and Varuna strutted like a prince in his wedding suit.
Everything went smoothly until the wedding bells rang, making the donkey
bride and groom start stomping and kicking. It took a snack from the
wedding feast to calm their nerves. When the party ended, the weather
forecast still said the sun would shine in the days ahead. But the villagers
went to bed happy and hopeful.

Donkey weddings are still quite rare. At the other end of India, in the
tea-producing state of Assam, there is a tribe of people who think donkey
marriages are downright silly. To pray for *their* monsoon rains every year,
they have frog weddings.

BEWARE OF PARROT

In the Ukrainian city of Izium, a retired policeman named Hennady lived quietly with his pet parrot. Too quietly. After living with the bird for a year, he still could not get the parrot to talk. No "pretty bird," no "Polly want a cracker," not a squawk. One day Hennady tipped his hat to his silent bird and headed out the door.

No sooner had he turned the corner when three bad Izium boys snuck up to the house. They peered through Hennady's window to make sure that he was gone. They wanted his brand new TV — and maybe the microwave

too. The boys pried open the window and all three jumped over the sill.
Suddenly a shrill voice rang out, "STOP! I'LL SHOOT!"

The burglars froze.

"ON THE GROUND!" the voice insisted. "ON THE GROUND!"

Immediately they dropped, bellies to the floor, hands behind their heads.

That's exactly how Hennady found the boys when he returned home—
foiled by his parrot, who had finally found his voice. Apparently, some quiet
parrots refuse to speak up until they have something important to say.

ACTING LIKE A PIG

Arne Braut raises pigs in Norway. So when he spotted a rubber pig mask
on his vacation, he bought it. Back on the farm, Arne put on the mask to
entertain his pigs. He grunted. He laughed. He grunted again. Arne always
knew that pigs were smart, but his pig imitations taught him something
new: pigs have a sense of humor. They got the joke. They gathered around
and snorted with pleasure.

Now Arne often wears his mask to chat with his pigs, and they've all
become much better friends. "Before, the pigs used to squeal and run away,"
says Arne. "Now they are calm and come up to me right away. The change
is incredible to see." And calmer pigs stay healthier. That's why officials in
Germany encourage pig farmers in their country to chat with their pigs every
day. Perhaps Arne can tell them where he bought his mask.

ELEPHANT DENTURES

Morakot is an elderly elephant. She lives in Thailand, where *morakot* means emerald. By the time she was eighty years old, Morakot had a problem—a jumbo problem. She was toothless. Elephants grow six sets of chewing teeth (called molars) in their lifetimes. When they grind down their last pair, they can't eat enough to live.

Morakot could barely munch mushy bananas. She grew so weak that her caretakers made a sling from a tree to support her. Then they asked Dr. Somsak, a veterinarian, for help. Dr. Somsak's solution: custom-made elephant dentures.

Each false molar was the size of a small brick. Two elephant handlers guided the teeth into place in Morakot's jaw. One sat on Morakot's back, moving the dentures with a string, while the other directed him from the ground. Within minutes Morakot was cheerfully chewing grass again. She may be the first elephant to get false teeth, but she won't be the last. Since he fitted Morakot, word has spread, and Dr. Somsak has received more requests for jumbo dentures from owners of other elderly elephants.

LAZY BIRDS HITCH A RIDE

Long ago, the northern bald ibis was easy to spot flying above the cliffs and coasts of Europe. But the funny-looking fowl was delicious to eat, and for hundreds of years people hunted so many bald ibises that the birds almost became extinct.

In the Austrian Alps, a team of ornithologists (scientists who study birds) were worried. They hated to see this rare bird disappear. One spring the ornithologists, Johannes, Angelika, Isabel, and Paul, took eggs from captive ibises in order to hatch a batch of babies who would learn to live in the wild.

Angelika and Isabel fed twenty-one hatchlings by hand, then watched them spread their wings and learn to fly. The baby ibises followed Angelika and Isabel everywhere, as if the scientists were their mothers.

The birds learned to eat bugs and frogs, but winter was approaching, and soon there wouldn't be any food in the frozen ground. They had to learn how to migrate—to fly south.

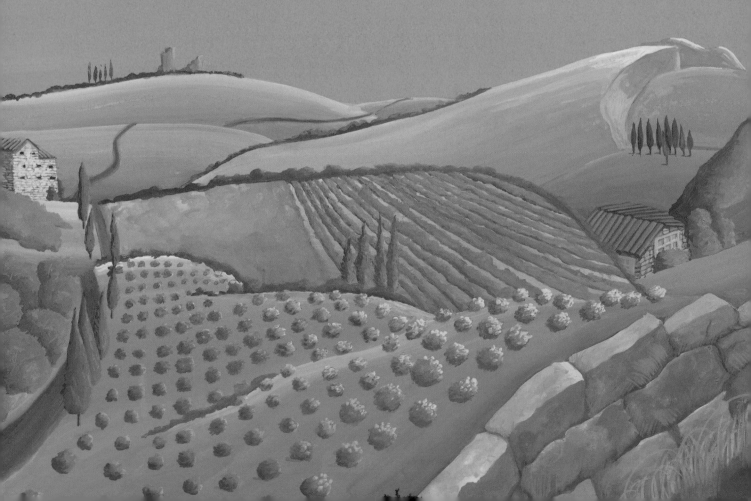

The scientists chose a pretty region in Italy called Tuscany and plotted a route. But birds don't read maps, and there were no bird parents to lead the way. So Johannes and Paul piloted two tiny aircraft called ultralights to guide those birds to Tuscany. Angelika and Isabel sat in the back, clucking, "Come, come . . . come, come." Twenty-one young birds looked into their adopted mothers' encouraging faces, stretched forty-two glistening black wings, and followed.

For a week, they flapped over the Alps, following the ultralights. But not far into Italy, one of the aircraft broke down. Then the tired ibises refused to budge. The scientists had to rent a car and hire a driver to take the flock the rest of the way. Now, those lazy birds rest for the winter under the Tuscan sun, then fly home to Austria in the spring. That is, when their instinct for flying—not driving—shifts into gear.

A HORSE IN THE HOUSE

Vikas Wavale and his wife, Sarika, wanted a house pet. They had no children and thought an animal might make life in their small apartment near Mumbai, India, more exciting.

So Vikas went to an outdoor market to find the perfect pet. When he saw Akash, he had to have him. Vikas didn't care what Akash cost and happily paid the seller 51,000 rupees (more than a thousand dollars). But Akash wasn't a perfect house pet at all. He was a horse.

When Vikas brought the horse home to live in his apartment, he and Sarika decided to move out—to give Akash more room. The horse had the house to himself.

The Wavales' friends and family were shocked. Vikas could not understand why. He assured them that the height of the apartment was just fine for Akash, who was not much more than five feet tall. "But once inside," said Vikas, "he doesn't get too much leg space to trot around."

Sarika agreed. She rides him outside every day, "to avoid muscle cramps."

Vikas and Sarika now live next door with Vikas's parents. The Wavale family has gotten used to the arrangement. But when Akash whinnies or snorts late at night, other people living nearby complain. Akash, on the other hand, has yet to gripe about the volume of the neighbors' TV or their choice of music.

STICKY BUSINESS

Tirto is usually ferocious. He's a Komodo dragon—the biggest kind of lizard in the world. He has a snakelike tongue, shark-sharp teeth, and an eight-foot-long body as powerful as a crocodile's. Komodo dragons love to eat meat. When they kill their prey, they swallow every last bit of bone and fur. This is not a beast you want to needle.

But Tirto was sick. He barely ate. Dr. Oh Soon Hock, the veterinarian at the Singapore zoo where Tirto lived, thought acupuncture might help. Acupuncture is an ancient Chinese treatment that pricks patients (usually human ones) with needles to change their energy flow. Dr. Oh (who has treated giraffes, cheetahs, and an orangutan, too) stuck extra-large steel needles into Tirto's thick, leathery skin.

It's hard to imagine that being pricked makes anyone feel better. But Dr. Oh says it doesn't hurt, "if you know what to do." Tirto wasn't cured immediately, but after his acupuncture, he was more active and seemed very relaxed. Apparently, needling was just what Tirto needed.

THE NEARSIGHTED GREYHOUND

Greyhounds love to chase rabbits. Unlike bloodhounds or bassets, who depend on their noses to follow a scent, greyhounds are "sight hounds"—they rely on their eyes. Farmers once kept greyhounds to hunt for jackrabbits that ruined their fields. But the farmers began to brag about whose dog was the fastest, and they started dog races to settle their bets.

Greyhound racing is now a professional sport. The dogs dash around a track trying to catch a mechanical hare. While the dogs simply enjoy the thrill of the chase, their owners hate to lose. In Manchester, England, one greyhound owner worried after each race. Her dog, Gus, loved running but was happy to finish in second place. What was preventing him from coming in first? In a tizzy, she brought Gus to England's best animal eye doctor—dog ophthalmologist Pip Boydell.

Dr. Boydell used special equipment to check Gus's vision and discovered that the pup needed glasses. He was nearsighted. "Although common in humans," said the veterinarian, "it's rare to find a dog with this condition." Then again, who ever really checks? Dogs don't usually read, or drive, or watch TV. Greyhounds, however, must see their quarry in order to chase it. This fuzzy-sighted fellow couldn't see past the dog in first place. As close as Gus got, he never tried to be first. He stayed behind to avoid getting lost.

Dr. Boydell fitted Gus with dog contact lenses. Immediately the world of that swift-footed, nearsighted greyhound took shape. Gus could see the horizon, the hare's tail ahead, and the look of surprise on the lead dog's face as he passed him to win race after race.

SPY KITTY

Today, special detective stores supply equipment for spying; they sell tiny video cameras shaped like alarm clocks or even tinier ones shaped like pens. But in the 1960s, only *real* spies had any technology for spying, and they had to invent it all themselves.

One special agent (his name is *still* top secret) thought cats were the sneakiest animals around: they can balance on ledges and see in the dark. Why not transform an ordinary house cat into an extraordinary spy kitty? The spy spent five years inventing a tiny listening device. Then a secret-agent veterinarian inserted it, very carefully, under a cat's fur and hid an antenna in its tail to transmit sounds as soft as whispers. They named the cat Acoustic Kitty.

Back then, American spies wanted to learn Russia's deepest secrets. By teaching Acoustic Kitty to snoop on windowsills or under tables in cafés, the spies thought they'd be able to catch Russian spies spilling clues (along with their crumbs). After weeks of training, the spies drove Acoustic Kitty to a park in Moscow near the Kremlin—the Russian capitol building. They pointed to two men on a bench and told Acoustic Kitty to listen to them and ignore the birds, the dogs, and the wind in the trees.

There's a saying, "You can't herd cats" (because cats do what they please). Acoustic Kitty was no exception. He jumped from the van, disappearing into traffic, and those spies never *heard* him (or herded him) again. Even today there's a top-secret report in America's spy files. It says that cats can be altered and trained to perform certain tasks, but for real spy missions, doing so "would not be practical."

OLD MAN MOM

A baby hippo and his mother were eating their breakfast of grass on the banks of the Sabaki River, when a tsunami—a giant wave—hit the coast of Kenya. The water rushed up the river, pushed the baby hippo off his feet, and whooshed him out to sea.

Hippos can swim, but they hate the ocean. Salt water dries out their skin, and they don't know how to surf. People on the shore saw the little hippo struggling in the waves and rescued him with a fishnet. They named him Owen and brought him to a nature preserve. Owen didn't know he was safe. In a panic, he ran to the first large gray animal he saw. It wasn't his mother. It wasn't even a hippo. It was an old tortoise named Mzee, which means "old man" in an African language, Swahili.

Mzee hissed. He was nearly one hundred years old—babies annoyed him. Owen didn't care. Mzee's round gray shell and wrinkly legs reminded Owen of his mother. Owen followed Mzee everywhere, and, surprisingly, the old tortoise soon stopped complaining.

Hippos adore company. They spend hours in mud ponds snuggling with friends. Now Owen rests his head on Mzee's shell and lovingly licks his face. They sleep together and go for swims. Park workers were delighted. "A mammal with a mammal—yes, it happens," said one of them. "But reptiles and mammals—we haven't seen this." As for Old Man Mzee, he seems happy now to be Old Man Mom.

BUSY BEAVERS

Five men splashed into a Louisiana creek: Sheriff Gun Ficklin, three deputies, and a lawyer. Following a tip, the lawmen were hunting for money bags. Three bags with thousands of dollars inside had been stolen from the Lucky Dollar Casino. They found two bags immediately. But, hard as they looked, the lawmen couldn't find the third. A pair of beavers watching from a distance were no help at all. The beavers were busy.

Wherever beavers find running water, they build dams, using twigs, mud, leaves, and whatever else they can grab. A deputy decided to drain the water to see what was at the bottom. He began to take down the dam twig by twig. And there, inside the dam, was the money. Those beavers had used it to plaster cracks, like very expensive papier-mâché. The owners of the Lucky Dollar Casino felt lucky indeed to get their money back—even if it *was* soggy.

SOMETHING TO CROW ABOUT

It's hard to know what a chicken is thinking. Chickens strut, cluck, and peck as a matter of course. When they act truly strange, farmers in Germany call on Dr. Barbara Luetzeler, one of the only chicken psychologists in the country (if not the world).

Dr. Luetzeler, who treats ducks and geese too, is famous for diagnosing the odd behavior of two thousand chickens who wobbled their heads in unison. She decided it was "motorway neurosis," caused by the whizzing noise of cars on a nearby highway. When the chickens were moved to a quiet spot, their strange head wobbling went away.

Then there was the case of a hen named Lucie. When the other young hens began to lay eggs, Lucie couldn't be bothered. Instead, she spent hours practicing her cock-a-doodle-doo. Perhaps she wanted a more glamorous job. After all, when the farm's rooster went to work each morning, he woke the sun. He turned on the day.

Lucie's farmer was alarmed, but he knew just what to do: he called the chicken doctor. Dr. Luetzeler told him that Lucie didn't need to be cured. Although unusual, acting like a rooster isn't harmful to a hen's health. Lucie soon got the knack of crowing at dawn. She "sounded a little hoarse," said Dr. Luetzeler, "but very proud."

MOOSE PADDLING

In Spokane, Washington, it's rare to see a moose on the loose. White-tailed deer, their impish cousins, frequently pop in uninvited. They sample vegetables growing in gardens and pull roses from bushes like children sneaking sugar flowers off the top of a cake. But moose are loners. They prefer privacy, which they usually find deep in the woods.

That's why Randi Longmeier was so surprised when she looked out the window and saw a big bull moose in her pool. She grabbed her video camera, and as it started to roll, the moose began to swim. With his huge antlers held high, he paddled to the deep end of the pool and back. It was

mid-August, after all, and he was hot. After his swim, he climbed from the shallow end, carefully stepped over the patio furniture, jumped the fence, and vanished into the woods.

Now, if the moose had caught television news that week, *he* would have been surprised. Stations all across the country broadcast the video of his little dip, but any moose could tell you that's not news. Moose are built for water; their nostrils close at will. They can eat plants from the bottoms of lakes without getting water up their moose noses, and they can easily swim ten miles, or even more, at a stretch.

FISHPOND 911

Leo Van Aert is not a superhero. But he knows how to save people in trouble. For years Leo sped through the streets of Antwerp, Belgium, driving an ambulance. When you're an ambulance driver, you move fast. Every second counts.

But now Leo is retired. He moves slowly and spends long afternoons outside raising fish in a small garden pond. Leo loves his fish—a kind of carp from Japan called koi. Some koi grow more than two feet long and live as long as fifty years.

One crisp autumn afternoon, Leo invited friends to his garden to celebrate his birthday. Suddenly, his wife ran over. One of Leo's fish was "acting funny," she said, flopping about frantically, then floating motionless. Leo the lifesaver kicked into gear.

He ran to the pond, took a look at his floundering fish, and thought, *Heart attack!* He grabbed the slippery koi from the water and massaged its heart. It didn't work. With no time to spare, Leo put his mouth over the koi's fish lips and began to blow—short, steady breaths, known as mouth-to-mouth resuscitation. After fifteen minutes, the fish wiggled.

Leo gently put the fish back into the pond. It flopped over and lay still again. Leo-the-fish-hero remained calm. "I again applied mouth-to-mouth and heart massages," he said. "That's when the fish recovered." Whenever Leo visits the garden now, that Belgian Japanese fish blows kisses.

A DAZZLING SNACK

There are safe ways to stash treasure—locked in a bank vault or buried on a desert island. Then there are crazy ways. Mr. Rajput, a diamond seller in Limbudi, India, hid his small bag of 1,722 glittering diamonds in a haystack. No one, he thought, would ever find them there.

No one, that is, but his hungry brown cow. When Mr. Rajput returned for his jewels, he found the cow chomping away and his diamonds devoured. Mr. Rajput and his staff hauled over buckets of grass, grain, and fruit. Day after day they stuffed the cow, waiting for her to poop.

After three days of sifting through stinky cow dung, the diamond-recovery team found only 310 gems. So Mr. Rajput brought the cow to the

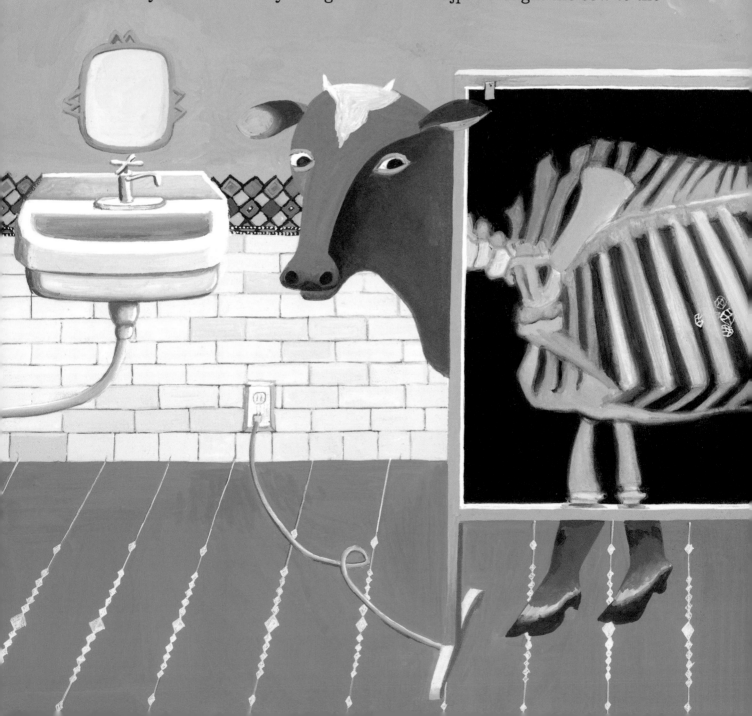

veterinarian and demanded medicine to speed up the process. "I'm sure within a week I will retrieve all my diamonds," he said.

The vet was not so sure. He told Mr. Rajput that a cow is a ruminant, which means that a cow stomach has four separate sections. Some diamonds might pass through all four sections. But the heavier and more valuable gems could sink and get stuck. They might be buried treasure forever.

No one feared that Mr. Rajput would take extreme measures to get his fortune back—because in India, cows are sacred. It's against the law to make them into steak.

AUTHOR'S NOTE

This book was Kathy's idea. She thought it would be fun to illustrate a book of amazing bird stories and began collecting newspaper articles like "Lazy Birds Take a Car" and "Beware of Parrot." When Kathy noticed extraordinary stories about other kinds of animals, she decided to cast a wider net. On the Internet, she sifted through hundreds of stories—from dogs that snore to bears that drink brandy. "Spy Kitty" was one of the first animal stories she chose to keep.

I'm a journalist, and as much as Kathy loves to paint, I love to write. When Kathy invited me to work on the book with her, we looked through her stash of articles and debated many points: for example, is brandy good for bears? (It's not.) Together, we chose sixteen stories that we both liked.

When an animal's behavior made me curious, I went to the Internet, looked through books, and called knowledgeable people, including a cow veterinarian and a parrot expert who answered my questions with great patience.

I also wanted to make sure the stories were true, so each of the stories has at least two sources. Some have as many as six. Many of the reports were found in newspapers from around the world. This is a partial list of story sources:

THE GREEN RABBIT

Cook, Gareth, and Tom Haines. "Cross Hare: Hop and Glow Mutant Bunny at Heart of Controversy over DNA Tampering." *Boston Globe,* September 17, 2000.

Copeland, Libby. "It's Not Easy Being Green; A Neon Bunny Spans and Divides Art and Science." *The Washington Post,* October 18, 2000.

THE DONKEY WEDDING

Deutsche Presse-Agentur. "Donkeys Married Off in Indian State to Appease Rain Gods." June 17, 2003.

Mathur, Meghana/Global News Wire. "Will It Rain Donkeys This Year? Bangalore Hopes So." *The Economic Times of India,* June 18, 2003.

BEWARE OF PARROT

Deutsche Presse-Agentur. "Ukrainian Parrot Foils Theft Attempt." October 6, 2003.

"Storyville." *Independent on Sunday* (London), October 12, 2003.

ACTING LIKE A PIG

Cukan, Alex/United Press International. "Things We Don't Understand." Jockstrip: The World As We Know It. October 29, 2002.

"In a Pig's Eye." First Light! Something Bright to Start Your Day. *Edmonton Sun* (Alberta, Canada), October 26, 2002.

ELEPHANT DENTURES

Global News Wire: Asia Africa Intelligence Wire, ONASA News Agency. "Thai Elephant Becomes World's First to Receive False Tooth." January 7, 2004.

"Jumbo Dentures for Ill Elephant Morakot." *The Nation* (Bangkok, Thailand), January 9, 2004.

LAZY BIRDS HITCH A RIDE

Tibbetts, Graham. "This Way, Baldie: Microlight Plays Mother to Teach Northern Bald Ibis to Migrate." *The Daily Telegraph* (London), August, 26, 2003.

Fritz, Johannes, Angelika Reiter, and Paul Fritz. "Return from Noah's Ark: Ultralight Planes Shall Teach a Group of Highly Endangered Waldrapp Ibises, *Geronticus eremita,* a New Migration Route From Austria to Italy." Ibis Project website: http://www.waldrappteam.at/.

A HORSE IN THE HOUSE

Natu, Nitasha. "This Horse Lives in a 200-sq-ft Chawl!" *Mid-day.com* (Mumbai, India), February 18, 2004. http://web.mid-day.com/.

"Couple Just Horsing Around." What in the Weird. *mX* Magazine, (Melbourne, Australia), February 19, 2004.

STICKY BUSINESS

Associated Press Worldstream. "Giant Komodo Dragon Receives Acupuncture Treatments for Nerve Problem." August 19, 2003.

THE NEARSIGHTED GREYHOUND

"A Greyhound Owner Was Shocked to Discover Why Her Prize Dog Kept Losing— He Needed Glasses!" *Sunday Times* (London), November 4, 2001.

Powell, Adam. "A Victory in Sight." *Daily Mail* (London), October 19, 2001.

SPY KITTY

Agence France Presse. "CIA Tried to Use Cat for Spying." September 11, 2001.

Central Intelligence Agency Memorandum, Document 27. March 1967. http://www2.gwu.edu/~nsarchiv/NSAEBB/NSAEBB54/.

OLD MAN MOM

"Strange Love of a Tortoise and the Orphan Hippo." *Africa News,* January 6, 2005.

Selva, Meera. "Owen the Baby Hippo Is Adopted by 100-Year-Old Giant Tortoise." *The Independent* (London), January 8, 2005.

BUSY BEAVERS

Associated Press. "Beavers Weave Stolen Cash into a Dam Near Baton Rouge." November 15, 2004.

Anderson, Bob. "Money Found at Dam: Beavers Use Bags Thrown into Creek." *The Advocate* (Baton Rouge, Louisiana), November 15, 2004.

SOMETHING TO CROW ABOUT

Moore, David. "Hen Out and Proud for Crowing Out Loud." *Townsville Sun* (Australia), September 27, 2003.

MOOSE PADDLING

"Moose Takes a Dip in Family Pool." *CNN Live Today,* CNN, August 16, 2001.

FISHPOND 911

Reuters. "Man Gives Koi Mouth-to-Mouth." November 4, 2003.

"Ex-Ambulance Driver Saves Fish with Kiss of Life." *Vancouver Sun* (British Columbia, Canada), November 6, 2003.

A DAZZLING SNACK

"Cow's a Real Gem" First Light! Something Bright to Start Your Day. *Edmonton Sun* (Alberta, Canada), January 19, 2004.

Agence France Presse. "Diamonds Are One Cow's Meal Ticket to Stardom in India." January 25, 2004.